The

by Iain Gray

PUBLISHING

WRITING *to* REMEMBER

Lang**Syne**

PUBLISHING

WRITING *to* REMEMBER

Strathclyde Business Centre
120 Carstairs Street, Glasgow G40 4JD
Tel: 0141 554 9944 Fax: 0141 554 9955
E-mail: info@scottish-memories.co.uk
www.langsyneshop.co.uk

Designed by Dorothy Meikle
Printed by Thomson Litho, East Kilbride
© Lang Syne Publishers Ltd 2006
ISBN 1-85217-229-0
ISBN 978-1-85217-229-9

The Moffats

MOTTO:
I hope for better things.

CREST:
A coronet and a cross.

TERRITORY:
Annandale.

Chapter one:

Origins of Scottish surnames

by George Forbes

It all began with the Normans.

For it was they who introduced surnames into common usage more than a thousand years ago, initially based on the title of their estates, local villages and chateaux in France to distinguish and identify these landholdings, usually acquired at the point of a bloodstained sword.

Such grand descriptions also helped enhance the prestige of these arrogant warlords and generally glorify their lofty positions high above the humble serfs slaving away below in the pecking order who only had single names, often with Biblical connotations as in Pierre and Jacques.

The only descriptive distinctions

among this peasantry concerned their occupations, like Pierre the swineherd or Jacques the ferryman.

The Normans themselves were originally Vikings (or Northmen) who raided, colonised and eventually settled down around the French coastline.

They had sailed up the Seine in their longboats in 900AD under their ferocious leader Rollo and ruled the roost in north east France before sailing over to conquer England, bringing their relatively new tradition of having surnames with them.

It took another hundred years for the Normans to percolate northwards and surnames did not begin to appear in Scotland until the thirteenth century.

These adventurous knights brought an aura of chivalry with them and it was said no damsel of any distinction would marry a man unless he had at least two names.

The family names included that of Scotland's great hero Robert De Brus and his compatriots were warriors from families like the De Morevils, De Umphravils, De Berkelais, De Quincis, De Viponts and De Vaux.

As the knights settled the boundaries of their vast estates, they took territorial names, as in Hamilton, Moray, Crawford, Cunningham, Dunbar, Ross, Wemyss, Dundas, Galloway, Renfrew, Greenhill, Hazelwood, Sandylands and Church-hill.

Other names, though not with any obvious geographical or topographical features, nevertheless derived from ancient parishes like Douglas, Forbes, Dalyell and Guthrie.

Other surnames were coined in connection with occupations, castles or legendary deeds. Stuart originated in the word steward, a prestigious post which was an integral part of any large medieval household. The same applied to Cooks, Chamberlains, Constables and Porters.

Borders towns and forts - needed in

areas like the Debateable Lands which were constantly fought over by feuding local families - had their own distinctive names; and it was often from them that the resident groups took their communal titles, as in the Grahams of Annandale, the Elliots and Armstrongs of the East Marches, the Scotts and Kerrs of Teviotdale and Eskdale.

Even physical attributes crept into surnames, as in Small, Little and More (the latter being 'beg' in Gaelic), Long or Lang, Stark, Stout, Strong or Strang and even Jolly.

Mieklejohns would have had the strength of several men, while Littlejohn was named after the legendary sidekick of Robin Hood.

Colours got into the act with Black, White, Grey, Brown and Green (Red developed into Reid, Ruddy or Ruddiman). Blue was rare and nobody ever wanted to be associated with yellow.

Pompous worthies took the name Wiseman, Goodman and Goodall.

Words intimating the sons of leading figures were soon affiliated into the language as in Johnson, Adamson, Richardson and Thomson, while the Norman equivalent of Fitz (from the French-Latin 'filius' meaning 'son') cropped up in Fitzmaurice and Fitzgerald.

The prefix 'Mac' was 'son of' in Gaelic and clans often originated with occupations - as in MacNab being sons of the Abbot, MacPherson and MacVicar being sons of the minister and MacIntosh being sons of the chief.

The church's influence could be found in the names Kirk, Clerk, Clarke, Bishop, Friar and Monk. Proctor came from a church official, Singer and Sangster from choristers, Gilchrist and Gillies from Christ's servant, Mitchell, Gilmory and Gilmour from servants of St Michael and Mary, Malcolm from a servant of Columba and Gillespie from a bishop's servant.

The rudimentary medical profession was represented by Barber (a trade which also once included dentistry and surgery) as well as Leech or Leitch.

Businessmen produced Merchants, Mercers, Monypennies, Chapmans, Sellers and Scales, while down at the old village watermill the names that cropped up included Miller, Walker and Fuller.

Other self explanatory trades included Coopers, Brands, Barkers, Tanners, Skinners, Brewsters and Brewers, Tailors, Saddlers, Wrights, Cartwrights, Smiths, Harpers, Joiners, Sawyers, Masons and Plumbers.

Even the scenery was utilised as in Craig, Moor, Hill, Glen, Wood and Forrest.

Rank, whether high or low, took its place with Laird, Barron, Knight, Tennant, Farmer, Husband, Granger, Grieve, Shepherd, Shearer and Fletcher.

The hunt and the chase supplied Hunter, Falconer, Fowler, Fox, Forrester, Archer and Spearman.

The renowned medieval historian Froissart, who eulogised about the romantic

deeds of chivalry (and who condemned
Scotland as being a poverty stricken waste-
land), once sniffily dismissed the peasantry of
his native France as the jacquerie (or the
jacques-without-names) but it was these same
humble folk who ended up overthrowing the
arrogant aristocracy.

In the olden days, only the blueblooded
knights of antiquity were entitled to full, proper names, both Christian and surnames, but
with the passing of time and a more egalitari-
an, less feudal atmosphere, more respectful
and worthy titles spread throughout the popu-
lace as a whole.

Echoes of a far distant past can still be
found in most names and they can be borne
with pride in commemoration of past generations who fought and toiled in some capacity
or other to make our nation what it now is, for
good or ill.

Chapter two:

Living on the frontline

There are two equally plausible explanations for the origin of the surname of Moffat, but whatever its origin, bearers of the name today can lay claim to a descent from one of the oldest and most famous – and frequently infamous – families of the Scottish Borders.

The Highlands and Islands had their closely knit communities of clans, with their own heritage and traditions, while the communities of families of the Borders were also fiercely proud of their own ancient homeland and glorious deeds and exploits.

No less so than with the Moffats, with the many branches of the family dominating the very landscape of the Borders for centuries.

One claim is that the progenitor, or 'name-father', of the Moffats was a Norman known as William de Mont Alto, who had settled in present day Annandale, in Dumfriesshire, at some stage in the tenth century.

This was at least 200 years before those Normans who had settled in England in the wake of the Norman Conquest of 1066 came north to settle in Scotland.

William de Mont Alto's name, it is claimed, gradually assumed the form of 'Moffat', after going through variations that included 'Montealt' and 'Movat', and it was through this that the town of Moffat acquired its name.

Another theory, however, is that rather than the town taking its name from someone who had settled there, the 'Moffats' took their name from the town itself.

According to this theory, 'Moffat' stems from the Scottish Gaelic 'magh fada', or the Irish Gaelic 'mai-fad', both meaning 'long plain', and the area in which Moffat lies certainly meets with this topographical description.

A confusing variety of forms of the name surfaced over the centuries, including Moffatt, Moffet, Moffett, Moffit, Maffat, Muffet, Morphit, Mufet, and Movat – and it is interesting to note that the most common spelling of the name today in Northern Ireland, where many 'Moffats' settled in the seventeenth century, is 'Moffett'.

As confusing as the variety of forms of the name is the rather bewildering genealogy of the Moffats, who appear to have been particularly virile and fertile considering the numerous branches of the family that were spawned over the centuries!

What was then the small hamlet of Moffat, in Annandale, was certainly the hub from which the family branched out.

A land charter in the barony of Westerkirk was granted to the family in 1300, while 260 years later no less than eleven branches of the family were recorded – including the Moffats of Wachopegill, Craigholm, Meckleholm, Ericstane, and Bludewise, and the prosperous lairds of Granton, Auldton, and Knock.

One of the earliest members of the family to be mentioned in the historical record is Nicholas de Mufet, who witnessed a charter by the Bishop of Glasgow in 1230, while he himself became bishop in 1268.

Known as the 'Laughing Archdeacon of Teviotdale', he died two years later, however, apparently without being officially consecrated, and one theory is that this was because he had refused to pay the Church in Rome the necessary fee for the honour.

Much of the high romance and drama associated with the Moffats begins with their involvement in Scotland's bitter and bloody Wars of Independence with its English neighbour.

Situated as they were on the Borders, the Moffats, in common with other Border families, were literally in the frontline of a conflict that frequently laid waste to their lands and possessions.

A Robert and a Thomas de Moffett were among the signatories in 1296 to a humiliating treaty of fealty, known as the Ragman Roll, to the conquering Edward I, known and loathed as the 'Hammer of the Scots'.

Signed by 1,500 earls, bishops, and burgesses, the parchment is known as the Ragman Roll because of the profusion of ribbons that dangle from the seals of the signatories.

With Scotland under the iron grip of English occupation at the time, those who signed had little option but to do so – but the humiliation was avenged when William Wallace sparked off a revolt in May of 1297, after slaying Sir William Heselrig, Sheriff of Lanark.

An expert in the tactics of guerrilla warfare, Wallace led his hardened band of freedom fighters, including the Moffats, on a series of lightning campaigns that inflicted stunning defeats on the English garrisons.

One of Wallace's many temporary headquarters was located in the near-impenetrable depths of what was then the great forest of Selkirk, and among his fellow 'bravehearts' were the Moffats, who knew every hidden pathway.

The Moffats are also on record for the vital role they played in 1297 in helping Wallace to set up an ambush by constructing a ditch deep enough to hide a man on horseback.

Wallace's campaigns culminated in the liberation of practically all of Scotland following

the battle of Stirling Bridge, on September 11, 1297, but defeat followed at the battle of Falkirk in July of the following year.

He was eventually betrayed and captured in August of 1305, and, on August 23 of that year, he was brutally executed in London on the orders of a vengeful Edward I.

Chained to a hurdle, he was dragged by horses from Westminster to Smithfield, where he then suffered the horrific fate of castration and disembowelment while still alive.

His genitals and entrails were burned before his eyes before his agony finally ended with a mighty stroke of the headman's axe.

As if this was not enough, his heart was then torn from his body and thrown into the flames, while his body was further butchered by being hacked into four pieces.

These four quarters were despatched to be put on display at Newcastle-on-Tyne, Berwick, Stirling, and Perth, while his head was mounted on a pike on London Bridge.

Edward had hoped that Wallace's gruesome fate would serve as an example to others and discourage further revolt against English occupation of Scotland, but it only served to further enrage and inflame patriotic passion.

Robert the Bruce, who was enthroned as King of Scots at Scone in March of 1306, took up the banner of revolt again and among his stalwart supporters were the Moffats.

It is known that Adam Moffat of Knock and his brother supplied forty of the skilled riders that made up the 500-strong Scottish light cavalry under the command of Sir Robert Keith at the battle of Bannockburn in June of 1314, when a 20,000-strong English army under Edward II was defeated by a Scots army less than half this strength.

By the midsummer of 1313 the mighty fortress of Stirling Castle was occupied by an English garrison under the command of Sir Philip Mowbray.

Bruce's brother, Edward, rashly agreed to a pledge by Mowbray that if the castle was not relieved by battle by midsummer of the following year, then he would surrender.

This made battle inevitable, and by June 23 of 1314 the two armies faced one another at Bannockburn, in sight of the castle.

It was on this day that Bruce slew the English knight Sir Henry de Bohun in single combat, but the battle proper was not fought until the following day, shortly after the rise of the midsummer sun.

The English cavalry launched a desperate but futile charge on the densely packed ranks of Scottish spearmen known as schiltrons, and by the time the sun had sank slowly in the west the English army had been totally routed.

At one crucial stage in the battle, English archers had been able to rain a deadly hail of arrows onto one of the Scottish divisions, and it was Sir Robert Keith and his light cavalry, including the Moffat contingent, that saved the day by charging the archers and dispersing them.

Chapter three:

Raiders of the West March

The Moffats acted for a time as trusted ambassadors for their country, with William de Moffete on record as having received a safe conduct pass from the English court in his role as the ambassador of Bruce's son and heir, David II.

In 1337, Walter de Moffet, the archdeacon of Midlothian, was appointed ambassador to the French royal court.

The Moffats were destined to fall from favour, however, and this was because of the lawless environment that frequently prevailed in the Scottish Borders.

They were among the feared body of families known as riding clans, or reivers, who took their name from their time-honoured custom of reiving, or raiding, not only their neighbours' livestock, but also that of their neighbours across the border.

The word 'bereaved', for example, indicating to have suffered loss, derives from the original 'reived', meaning to have suffered loss of property.

A constant thorn in the flesh of both the English and Scottish authorities was the cross-border raiding and pillaging carried out by well-mounted and heavily armed men, the contingent from the Scottish side of the border known and feared as 'moss troopers.'

In an attempt to bring order to what was known as the wild 'debateable land' on both sides of the border, Alexander II of Scotland had in 1237 signed the Treaty of York, which for the first time established the Scottish border with England as a line running from the Solway to the Tweed.

On either side of the border there were three 'marches' or areas of administration, the West, East, and Middle Marches, and a warden governed these.

Complaints from either side of the border

were dealt with on Truce Days, when the wardens of the different marches would act as arbitrators.

There was also a law known as the Hot Trod, that granted anyone who had their livestock stolen the right to pursue the thieves and recover their property.

The post of March Warden was a powerful and lucrative one, with rival families vying for the position, and the marches became virtually a law unto themselves.

In the Scottish borderlands, the Homes and Swintons dominated the East March, while the Armstrongs, Maxwells, Johnstones, and Grahams were the rulers of the West March – the ancient homelands of the Moffats.

The Kerrs, along with the Douglases and Elliots, held sway in the Middle March.

Wardens from the East Marches met at Redden Burn, on the Tweed, just west of Wark, while wardens for the Middle Marches met at Deadwater, on the North Tyne.

A record exists from 1398 of an agreement between commissioners for Scotland and

England that the men of Nithsdale, Galloway, Crawfordmuir, and Annandale – home of the Moffats – should meet the wardens of the West March at the 'Clochmabanstane' for redress.

Also known as the Lochmaben Stone, or the Clochmaben Stone, the Moffats would have been frequent visitors to this granite bulk, situated about a mile southwest of Gretna, on a small rise of ground at the head of the Solway Firth, at Sulwath.

By 1504, the Moffats appear to have still been in royal favour, because two men were hanged in the Borders for the murder of Thomas Moffet, described as one of the king's liegemen, or trusted officials, despite the fact that many of his relations were still notorious reivers.

One of the Moffats' most powerful enemies were the Johnstones of the West March who, in 1557 exacted a murderous retribution on the family by killing Robert Moffat, the family chief, and several of his kinsfolk by setting fire to a building in which they had gathered.

By May of 1583 two Moffats incurred

the wrath of the authorities for crimes that included fire-raising and murder, while in the same year a Gilbert Hay of Monkstown is on record as complaining of how a band of Moffats had raided his lands, leaving a trail of devastation in their pillaging wake.

Four years later, in 1587, the Scottish parliament declared the Moffats to be 'an unruly clan of the Western Marches', while in 1594 the parliament drew up a series of harsh measures 'to suppress the lawless Moffats and other Border clans.'

The lawless state of affairs was no better by 1608, however, when a Privy Council report graphically described how the 'wild incests, adulteries, convocation of the lieges, shooting and wearing of hackbuts, pistols, lances, daily bloodshed, oppression, and disobedience in civil matters, neither are nor has been punished.'

The final death knell for the Moffats was finally sounded in 1609, however, when a special commission set up by James VI arranged that many of the lands the family had held for centuries should be sold off to their bitter enemies, the Johnstones.

Many Moffats remained in the Borders, but many others were dispersed and sought a new life elsewhere.

Some of the lands lost to the Moffats were re-purchased by their descendants in the early years of the twentieth century.

The family's proud heritage was recognised in 1983 when Major Francis Moffat of Craigbeck was recognised by the Lord Lyon King of Arms of Scotland as hereditary clan chief, with the designation of Moffat of that Ilk.

Following his death in 1992, his daughter succeeded to the title as Madame Jean Moffat of that Ilk.

'I hope for better things' is the motto of the Moffats, while the crest is a coronet and cross.

Chapter four:

International renown

Generations of Moffats have achieved recognition in a diverse number of fields.

James Moffat, born in 1870, was the Scottish ecclesiastical historian who translated the Bible into modern English, while Robert Moffat, born in Ormiston, East Lothian, in 1795, was a missionary and explorer whose fame has largely been overshadowed by that of his son-in-law, the missionary David Livingstone.

Recognised as the 'father' and founder of missionary work in South Africa, Moffat also translated the Bible into the language of the natives of the former Bechuanaland, in addition to trekking across vast distances of previously uncharted territory, including 700 miles of the Kalahari Desert in 1854.

Moffat, whose daughter Mary married Livingstone in 1844 after meeting her at her father's missionary station in Kuruman, was also responsible for introducing the use of fertilisers and irrigation to his flock.

He also once temporarily abandoned his Christian principles to buy firearms with which to protect his flock from the warlike Zulus.

On the battlefield, Martin Moffat, born in Sligo, Ireland, in 1884, won a Victoria Cross for his gallantry in action on the Western front in 1918.

On the tennis court, Billie Jean Moffat is the maiden name of Billie Jean King, born in 1943 in Long Beach, California.

Inducted into the International Tennis Hall of Fame in 1987, she won the first of her six titles at Wimbledon in 1966, a venue where she eventually amassed no less than a total of six singles titles, ten women's doubles titles, and four mixed doubles titles.

An advocate against sexism in both sport and society in general, she is also the proud holder of twelve Grand Slam single titles, fourteen Grand Slam women's doubles titles, and eleven Grand Slam mixed doubles titles.

On the stage, Graham Moffat, born in

London in 1920, was a comedy film actor who
starred in several films with the great comedy
actor Will Hay, while Tracey Moffat, born in
1960, is the Australian artist best known for the
use of photography and video in her work.

His book *Arthur and the Lost Kingdoms*,
first published in 1999, puts forward the intrigu-
ing theory that King Arthur of 'Knights of the
Round Table' tradition was actually a prince of a
southern Scottish tribe.

In the world of broadcasting, Alistair
Moffat, born in the Scottish Borders in 1950, is a
writer and broadcaster.

Born in Paisley in 1961, Steven Moffat is
a comedy and drama writer for television whose
credits include BBC2's *Coupling* sitcom, while
Peter Moffat, born in 1923 is a British television
director whose many credits include the *Dr Who*
television series.

Most of us, meanwhile, can recall the
childhood nursery rhyme 'Little Miss Muffet',
but what is not commonly known is that the
Miss Muffet in question was actually the step-

daughter of a Dr Thomas Muffet, born in 1553, and who achieved acclaim as an expert in the study of spiders!

Moffat is also the name of a county in the U.S. State of Colorado, and was named after David H. Moffat, an immensely wealthy railroad tycoon who died in 1911.

The most famous 'Moffat', however, is the town itself, from where the proud family of Moffats themselves originate.

Situated in lovely countryside about 21 miles from the town of Dumfries, this spa town has attracted hordes of tourists from the early years of the nineteenth century onwards.

These have included the biographer James Boswell and, in 1817, no less a dignitary than the Grand Duke Nicholas of Russia, during his Grand Tour of Europe.

He was so impressed by the welcome he received that he insisted on paying double the amount on his hotel bill!

Not quite as wealthy as the Grand Duke was another famous visitor, Scotland's national bard, Robert Burns.

The poet had taken some refreshment in the Black Bull Hotel, which survives as the town's oldest such establishment, and it was here that he etched on a window the memorable lines:

Ask why God made the gem so small, and why so huge the granite – because God meant mankind should set the higher value on it.